Empowered Loving

A Guide To Learning
and Growing
Through Relationships

By Shems Heartwell

With Artwork by
Visionary Watercolor Artist
Meganne Forbes

Appreciations

Many thanks to Gay and Katie Hendricks for their amazing pioneering, modeling and teaching in the field of conscious relationships. Thank you to the many teachers and friends who have influenced and supported my journey. I am grateful to the work of JoAnna Chartrand and Dr. Dyrian Benz at the Relational Constellations Institute of California, truly profound and sacred to learn from both of you!

I send much respect and gratitude for my ancestors and family. Thank you, Lamara, for all of the learning and growing together, along with the graceful unweaving of our marriage. And I bow to the beauty, blessings and challenges that have provided the fertile ground for my learning, healing and discoveries.

A Special Gift To You

Visit my website now and receive a free short video series: "3 Key Skills That Will Revitalize and Transform Your Relationships"

shemsheartwell.com/loving

Praise for Empowered Loving

"A beautiful, heart-centered book that offers clear and simple guidance to empowered relationships and a freer, happier, and more loving life. I have experienced Shems' work personally and highly recommend him. "

- Jim Dreaver, Author of End Your Story, Begin Your Life

"What a beautiful and heartwarming book. The bright heart of Shems shines through all of these pages. There is much good, solid guidance in this inspired writing and I found many gems of practical wisdom touching and informing me. There is much explicit and helpful Information here that is presented in a straight-forward and applicable way. The phenomenal artwork included compliments the writing well. Thank you Shems for creating such a visionary and practical work."

- Dr. Dyrian Benz and JoAnne Chartrand, Authors of The Delight of Love & Belonging with Relational Constellations

"Empowered Loving, is a great practical guide and introduction to the foundational principles of creating conscious and meaningful relationships. It is a wealth of insights and reminders into how to make every moment of interaction with life rich and rewarding. Whether you are well read in these topics or exploring them for the first time this book has something of immense value to offer. "

- Logan Griffin, Energy Healer and Life Coach

In a very elegant and clear presentation Shems honors what he has learned from Gay and Katie Hendricks and other masters in the field of relationship. This is a lovely offering that synthesizes the key challenges to conscious relationship and how to navigate them. I like how Shems encourages us to pay attention to what is holding us back and with awareness keep practicing love.

- Tomas Heartfield, Co-director for Talking Hearts Counseling

Foreword

By Justin Faerman

Much has been written about love over the course of human history, the vast majority of which concerns romantic love, which although beautiful and empowering in it's own right, is only a fragment of the full spectrum of love we are capable of as humans. Romantic love is an echo of unconditional love, which is our most divine and evolved attribute and the state of being to which we all yearn to return, whether or not we are consciously aware of it.

We yearn for unconditional love from the people and world around us, yet is not something someone else can give us. It is something you must cultivate within yourself -- the process of which heals all wounds (spiritually, emotionally, mentally and physically), destroys all barriers to the abundance and freedom which are your birthright and brings about an enlightened state of peace, fulfillment and joy which most can only dream of. This is the reality that awaits anyone who is able to tear down the walls within themselves to reveal their true nature, which is existing in a state of unconditional love for all things.

This book is about 'Empowered Love', which, as I interpret it, is a way of engaging with yourself and the people in your life for maximum harmony and fulfillment, based solidly on practices, principles and understandings which are designed to take you ever closer to the state of unconditional love that is your essence. In it, you will learn the what, how and why of becoming more loving and aware in your everyday life. You will learn how to connect more deeply, authentically and passionately with yourself and the people and world around you. You will come to understand what has been keeping you from this blissful experience and what you can do to quickly and effectively change those old patterns which no longer serve your highest good. And ultimately, you will be given the keys to understanding your mind, body, spirit and emotions at a profound level, the experience of which will be liberating to you in many ways on all levels of your being.

If this book has found it's way into your hands, consider yourself blessed. You are about to take the next step in your conscious evolution -- one that will lead you to a deep and beautiful place within yourself that you may have forgotten existed, but are on the precipice of rediscovering.

I can think of few people I know who embody what they teach as authentically as Shems Heartwell and you are lucky to have him as your guide on your journey towards a more empowered way of living and loving. His wisdom and knowledge are timeless and his words resonate with truth and the first-hand experience of what he teaches. You are in good hands.

- Justin Faerman, Artist, Healer, Coach, Conscious Entrepreneur

Table of Contents

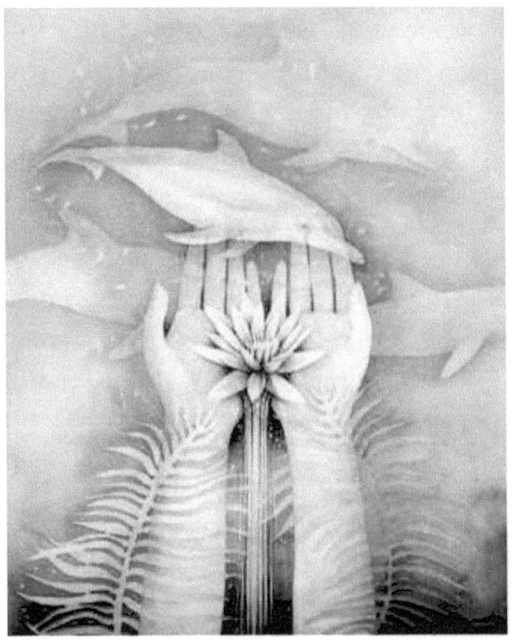

Empowered Loving

We each wield a great power that has the potential to radically transform our lives and the world around us. You know what it is. The ones, who have plugged into it, have made big waves in the world through their thoughts, words and actions. It is not special and yet it is the most rare and precious thing on the planet. It is an unlimited resource like the sun, but the clouds and storms of life can dampen its warmth and radiance. Yet it is always here, unwavering when we are open to it.

Love is the most beautiful thing that we can embody in this life. It is our power and the foundation of our purpose.

In every interaction, we have the opportunity to bring forth this precious gift through our hearts, eyes and hands. Let's make the choice together, to wash away whatever has been in the way of this force of life and choose to use each opportunity we have to empower our loving.

Our relationships are the ultimate fertile ground for this practice. Nowhere else will we find a more consistent place to see the shadows and the light reflect across our faces, inviting us into the unloved places, with the opportunity to integrate and heal them.

Love has the power to bring up any and everything that has ever been in the way of it's full expression. Any ways that we have ever shut out love come into the light when we are ready and willing to see.

Learning Along The Way

We grow up learning a lot about writing, reading, and arithmetic, but where was the curriculum for love, intimacy and relationships? What would you say is most valuable in your life? Does it matter if you know how to solve equations and write letters when at a deeper level you feel shut down, emotionally upset or overwhelmed with life's challenges?

When you have closed your heart to another in the grips of a challenging moment, wouldn't it be powerful to know how to face your fears, put down any defenses, and be able to navigate through stormy situations with confidence?

Relationships can be a fast track to healing and spiritual evolution, or a consistent challenge that slowly numbs and shuts us down over time. The passion and brightness of a new relationship wakes and inspires us, but then the deeper layers of our unconscious behaviors and conditioning begin to get in the way. Unless we learn how to transform these patterns, we will recycle them over and over again.

Connecting in partnership and choosing to deepen in love and intimacy is one of the most beautiful gifts and challenges of life. It gives us the opportunity to transform the past through the present experience of loving. Any challenge that arises in intimacy is an opportunity to heal and grow. We each have emotional edges from past experiences that can be smoothed out or sharpened depending on how willing we are to stay open to love and put our defenses down.

The solution to the challenges we face in relationships is for us to empower our loving. We do this by learning how to embrace and transform the unconscious patterns that limit our capacity to deeply connect. Our loving must become a conscious intentional practice. We each carry our own issues that get perfectly triggered by our loved ones and most people have been conditioned to avoid or numb out the problems.

This is a choice point. At some time in our lives we realize that our past conditioning is getting in the way of what we most want. This is when we can choose to bring light and awareness to the beliefs and behaviors that sabotage our life and relationships.

Here is where you may face the story or belief that change is hard or I can't change, this is just how I am. Everything changes and it is not true that change is difficult. What is difficult is to look at our shadows with a willingness to lovingly accept them and allow them to change. To be willing to put down our armoring and risk being in the unknown of vulnerability is one of the greatest strengths we can develop. If you are brave enough to allow change, then relationships and life can be a much more friendly playground.

I have experienced change as my greatest ally in learning how to adapt and fully appreciate what is here now. When a wildfire burned our home, my wife and I experienced a snowball of change that went on for years and it seemed like the fire was never going to go out. We lost our dogs within a year of the fire and went through many big hurdles during the building of our new home. The final kicker was my wife meeting another man and having that connection slowly unweave our marriage and catapult us both into new frontiers of love and letting go. From my vantage point now, I could not have experienced a more perfect journey to prepare me to be writing this book from the heart of my experiences.

Emerging

I believe that we are each here to blossom into the full potential of our beings. The essential self, when truly understood, is already perfect. Just as the acorn contains the oak, the essential self has everything it needs to fulfill its higher purpose. And when the inner conditions are right, it naturally emerges. These inner conditions are the soil of acceptance, love and the ability to fully tap into the full spectrum of our experience.

Contrary to what many of us have been taught, true love is an inner experience that radiates outward into the world. There is not an ideal person who will fulfill a void or lack of love inside. When we feel a longing for love and companionship, the first most important step is to activate our own inner lover. This is the most effective way to attract and sustain a healthy relationship. Our capacity to love and accept ourselves equals how much love we can give and receive from others.

Relationships help us to uncover more of who we already are. There is never a danger of attracting the wrong experience. Because, rather than trying to attract something we think we're missing, we attract the perfect conditions for our own growth and maturation. These conditions are reflected in the ones we love and the people we do not love. People show up perfectly into our lives in ways that will surface up whatever is in the way of the full maturation of our souls.

As I reflect on my marriage and past relationships, I can see how each partner has been a powerful catalyst for my healing and growth. Especially in my most venerable or frustrated moments, I look back and see where I had an opportunity to ask for what I want or to face a deep fear from the past. I don't see relationship challenges or heartbreaks as mistakes; I see them as opportunities for healing and claiming greater responsibility for our lives.

Beneath the surface of our resistances, discomforts and challenges are the inherent gifts and pure essence of our being. Our deepest hurts and wounds can be the catalysts of profound growth and healing when we meet them with loving arms and an open heart.

Core Issues

Anytime in our lives, particularly during developmental years, that we have experienced or perceived an interruption in the flow of love toward us can leave an emotional or psychological imprint. This imprint can show up in many ways and often feels like a need for love or attention or a fear of love and attention. Each of us may have many past impressions that are still influencing, often in subtle ways, our behaviors, beliefs and especially the depth of our intimate connections.

Most everyone has at least one core issue when it comes to relationships. The core issue may be invisible to you, but deeply affects how you connect to your partner or potential partners. Your core issue is an experience that comes up over and over in relationships that feels familiar and can hurt deeply. It is the one thing that you dread other people will either do to you or deny you. Or it is the thing you fear others will think about you or the way they will perceive you. It is rooted in a deep fear from past experience or conditioning that you would like to get rid of, avoid or not feel.

A core issue does not feel as if it comes from you. Instead it feels like something that keeps happening to you. When it happens to you, it triggers an emotional storm that leads to reaction, protection and defensiveness. It can cut you to your very core and can leave you feeling angry, resentful, devastated or withdrawn and numb. Either way, Core issues stimulate a dynamic of perpetrator and victim until we bring them to the light of conscious attention.

It can be difficult to understand that the thing you feel other people are doing to you is actually your own issue. It is much easier to believe that what's happening to you is somehow out of your control and the responsibility of others.

Here Is What Is Actually Happening

Each of us had various experiences in our family bonding and developmental years that influenced our comfort with intimacy, as well as our beliefs and attitude. Past emotional experiences, imprints and traumas from our childhood have left residue in our bodies and psyche. These past experiences are like undigested food lying dormant, awaiting the right circumstances to allow them to surface up to be metabolized and integrated.

What is really fascinating is that we literally attract the perfect people and situations that will help us to resolve these past experiences. We all do this, but not consciously!

We are like cells with receptor sites that are magnetizing the perfect cells that will come to us and activate our unprocessed issues. This is a brilliant aspect of humanity, and it works very well when we are aware of this functioning of the universe and are able to use these opportunities to heal and transform our lives. Obviously, it does not work when we have learned to be defensive, distract ourselves or avoid the issues that are arising.

Where Do These Issues Come From?

In an ideal world, we would have all received the perfect recipe of nurturance, healthy bonding and conscious parenting. Imagine if your family modeling and experience was like this:

- You were brought up with two parents who role-modeled taking 100 percent personal responsibility for their own feelings, neither of them blamed each other or turned to addictions to avoid their discomfort or feelings.

- Both of your parents were open to learning when conflict arose. Neither of them got angry or withdrew in conflict and they were both willing to learn and grow from their experience.

- Your parents were openly affectionate with each other.

- Your parents laughed and played with each other, obviously delighting in each other's company.

- Your parents supported each other in their highest good and in being vulnerable.

- Both of your parents were loving and consistently available for you, supporting you in fulfilling your highest potential. You felt valued by them and important to them.

Most likely, you did not experience much of the above role modeling. Even with the best intentions, our parents had their own social and family conditioning that influenced their ability to parent and sustain a healthy relationship with each other. Add in siblings, financial pressures and various stresses and it makes it hard for anyone to be patient and loving under the pressures of life.

You might have been brought up in a single-parent household so you didn't see a loving relationship role modeled. Or, if you had two parents or caregivers, you may have experienced them:

- Blame each other or you for their painful feelings - not being there for themselves, each other or you.

- Turn to various addictions such as food, alcohol, drugs, TV, work, spending, anger and so on, to avoid feeling and taking responsibility for their feelings.

- Use anger, withdrawal, resistance and/or giving up to control each other or avoid conflict.

- Not knowing how to lovingly resolve conflict due to being closed to learning from each other.

- Not being there for each other emotionally. Not supporting each other's highest potential.

- Not laughing, playing or showing much affection with each other or with you.

- Not being there to love and support you in your discussions. Instead, you might have felt rejected and/or overly controlled by them.

How familiar does any of the above feel to you? Did you receive more modeling from the first list or the second list? The role modeling that you experienced is likely a mixture of both lists and there is a good chance that the second list is closer to your childhood reality.

You might be treating yourself the way your parents or caregivers treated themselves and/or you, and therefore you may have patterns of abandoning yourself as they abandoned you or themselves. You might have a fear of intimacy, stemming from fears of rejection and/or of control stemming from your parents or caregivers being rejecting and/or overly controlling with you. You might get immediately triggered into anger, withdrawal, compliance or resistance when conflict arises, creating a situation where conflict doesn't get resolved.

Your relationship can be a valuable arena to learn to move from the second list to the first list -- if you and your partner are willing to do your inner healing work. But if you have the expectation that your relationship should be easy, then you might move on if it is hard, only to discover that the next one and the one after that, and so on, are also burdened with the same difficulties.

If you have an easy relationship that has maintained passion, aliveness, connection, joy, fun and play, you are very fortunate. Some people have an easy relationship because they settle for less than intimate connection, passion and aliveness. They avoid conflict and settle for peace and companionship, which is fine, if this is what both people want. But if you want a relationship that maintains deep emotional and physical connection, a relationship where you rarely feel lonely with each other, a relationship that is always evolving and growing toward deeper intimacy, then you need to be willing to heal your own issues first.

The journey toward wholeness and deeper sharing of love begins here. Our issues are our shadows. And, when we face our shadows, without judgment and resistance, the light of our awareness transforms them. Your willingness to look into the mirror of life and relationship will give you endless opportunities to empower your loving.

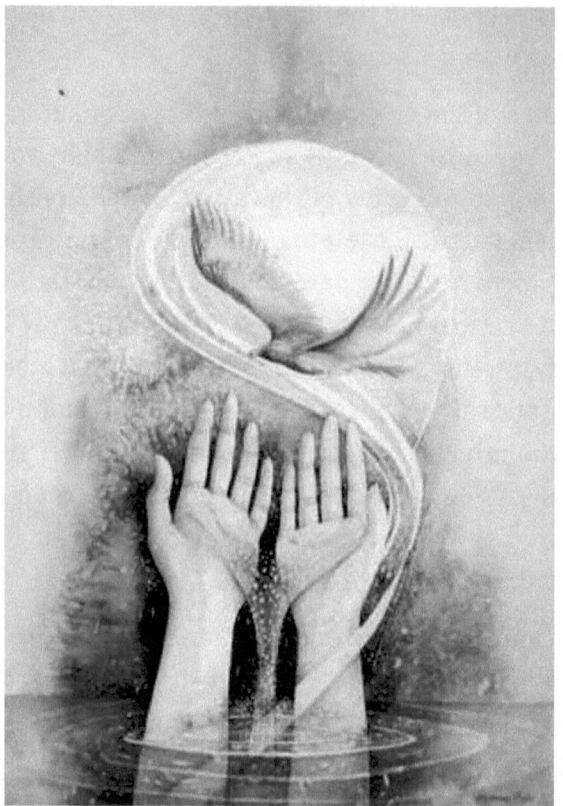

Making Your Loving Conscious

Every relationship in my life changed for the better when I became aware of how often I was withholding my inner experience. I had a lot of internal dialog that I was holding in and not expressing. What I began to discover was that my lack of expression created disconnection from the people I wished to be close with. I also started to notice that holding back my feelings and thoughts lead to a hyperactive mind and a disconnection from my heart and body intelligence. Honestly, I was a bit crazy inside when I was not authentically expressing my experience. I was bottled up and fizzy, ready to blow my lid.

Expression is a vital aspect of relating. Who does not love good music, theatre and art? The movement of our inner experience being brought out and witnessed can be a profound bridge for connection and mutual understanding.

How we express our thoughts and emotions is just one of many ways to make our loving more conscious. There are many more and each is important to understand if you truly wish to empower your loving. Take a moment to ask yourself these questions to get a sense of how evolved you are in your relationship skills:

- Is it easy for you to express love and appreciation?

- Are you fully honest and authentic with your communication, revealing your fears, judgments and vulnerability?

- Do you take full responsibility for your part in the challenges that arise, seeing that it takes "two to tango"?

- Do you ever withhold or resist love and intimacy with your partner?

- Are you easily defensive when receiving feedback or criticism?

- Do you blame your partner or situation for the difficulties in your life?

- Do you carry guilt or shame about something you have done or are not doing in your relationship?

- Do you notice that the fire of passion in your life and love has dwindled or gone out?

Being willing to honestly explore these questions is a doorway into greater responsibility and empowerment. If asking any of these questions brings up judgment, discomfort or resistance, the work has begun. Our inner thoughts and judgments are actually the cause of most relationship challenges. Issues with our loved ones often appear to be their stuff, but the truth is that what we react to in another has deeper roots in how we feel about and treat our own precious selves'. It may be tempting to want to evaluate your partner but I encourage you to put your attention on yourself first. My number one intention here is for you is to become the person who judges you the least and loves you the most. This is the fast track to loving others.

The following chapters are pieces to the puzzle that, when put together, support us in creating rewarding and successful relationships that grow deeper as they mature. There are exercises in some of the chapters intended to help integrate the information. It is not enough to understand this material logically. We must transfer this information into an embodied experience in which we are living and responding from. Understanding is simply the beginning.

With practice, we are able to allow our experience to guide us more than our thoughts and understanding. What

I mean by experience is our felt sense of knowing and the information that we receive through our body wisdom and emotional states. What we are feeling is often a more accurate guide than what we are thinking. When in doubt, take a moment to slow down and listen to your body. Become aware of where you may be holding tension or resistance and allow space to feel and be with your present experience. There is a reliable wisdom here that will over time become a trusted friend.

Practice Loving Fully

The best way to succeed at anything is to practice. With love, that means you practice the actual art of keeping good feelings flowing, so when you do hit a challenge, you're already adept at knowing how to steer your relationship into harmony again. Loving is being present and honest, not just being affectionate and nice! Being loving is about choosing to stay connected and present through the waves of challenge and resistance. Taking a moment to pause, breathe and become aware of what is happening is a loving and healing choice, especially in the middle of an emotional storm.

Love is and must be a practice. Through practice, love deepens. And it deepens in ways that will continually enrich and support you. There is always room to go deeper, no matter where you are in your relationship.

If you're single, then focus on self-love and acceptance, which will prepare you for a significant relationship. In many ways you are only in a relationship with your inner self anyway. The other person is often reflecting the thoughts and attitude that you have about yourself. If you pay close attention, you may notice we are each relating with all of the thoughts and reactions that are going on in our minds about the other person.

This is why it is essential to become aware of our thought patterns and to choose to dis-identify from the critical thoughts and self doubts that pollute our minds. Most of the thoughts that we think come through the filter of past experiences and conditioning. When you observe the thoughts and reactions that are going on in your mind, you can question whether they are truly accurate and valid in this moment or situation. The witness that is aware of and observing your thoughts is your essential self. This is where authentic love comes from. When you witness your thoughts with loving attention, you break the cycle of identifying with the limiting stories from the past.

Do not wait for your partner to be receptive to your love or for them to be loving to you first. Love opens up to more love. You can choose in any moment, regardless of what is happening in a situation, to turn on love and appreciation. This can be the most difficult thing to do when we are triggered and upset; however it is often the most effective way to transform a negative situation. Below the surface of any reactions or defenses is the loving presence of your essential self, much like the calm waters below the stormy surface of the ocean.

Begin With Yourself

If sending out loving attention and energy to your partner is difficult, then feel love inside and for yourself. Give yourself loving acceptance and care, not to avoid feelings of hurt or other emotions that may be activated, but to also feel loving energy along with whatever other feelings you may be experiencing. I am not a fan of getting rid of or overpowering negative or painful emotions, but rather favor fully feeling them to completion. Emotions are energy that is in motion and when they are suppressed or denied, we build up tension and stress.

When we are feeling triggered or reactive, it is most often from an un-integrated or wounded part within us that has not received attention or love. No one else can give us the attention and love that was needed when we first felt hurt, unloved or disconnected from our parents or friends. There is often a feeling of need or longing for support from another in relationship that comes from an attempt to get what we did not receive when we were young. Ultimately, what is most needed is a willingness to love and accept all of the parts of ourselves. What was not loved, approved of or accepted when we were young, is still looking for it from a source outside of oneself.

This is why our partner's attention, love or approval is only a temporary Band-Aid over what is ultimately our own responsibility to give to ourselves. Our partner's love can be hugely supportive and healing, benefitting our lives in beautiful ways, but it will not ultimately give us what we need. How fully we can receive the support and love from others is a reflection of our capacity to love our own self.

Feel Love All the Way Through

Love is a felt experience that grows with attention. Take a moment to let your body relax as much as possible. Breathe into your belly and think of what love feels like inside of you. When have you felt the greatest love within you and imagine feeling that again right now. Allow yourself to relish the experience and sensations of love. Let it permeate all the cells of your being. Allow it to move you in ways that surprise and nourish you. When we deeply feel love and allow it to blossom in our felt experience, it elicits a whole cascade of hormones and physiological processes that heal and feed our bodies, hearts and souls. This in turn allows us to bond more deeply with our beloved. Bonding in love builds a beautiful bridge that transforms feelings of separation. It helps us to experience compassion and connection with all of life.

Allow yourself to stretch out the length of time that you feel the sensations of love and connection. This is part of the practice of loving. Be spacious in the time that you are connecting and feeling. (At first this may not be easy, it is often easier for women than men, but it is highly worth the effort.) Going beyond the familiar and comfortable leads to new frontiers that light up more of our brain centers and consciousness. There is no juicier place to explore new frontiers than in an intimate loving relationship. And beginning within your own self is the fastest way to expanding love with another.

Emotional Intelligence

Emotional Intelligence is the ability to understand, manage, and effectively express one's own feelings, as well as being able to engage and navigate successfully with the feelings of others. Emotional Intelligence is absolutely essential in the formation, development and sustainability of relationships.

To be able to communicate clearly, we must be able to process and be with our own discomforts and emotions, so they don't overwhelm us and affect our ability to connect. Often, we try to avoid or deny our feelings with rationalization's or behaviors that suppress what is naturally occurring to help us heal and grow. This is a deeply ingrained social behavior that is not always easy to be aware of. When we suppress or disassociate from our emotional intelligence we also lose our physiological feedback system and ultimately, our ability to truly relate and connect with our self and others.

To be effective in feeling our emotions, we need to shift out of the thinking and rationalization part of our brains and focus attention on our experience and the sensations in our bodies. Once we shift out of our mental assessments and judgments, we can focus on the breath and the sensations that we are experiencing. Bringing attention home to your inner experience builds a fire of transformational presence. This presence of inner attention will burn up old pain and learned behaviors that interrupt true connection and intimacy.

Over a period of many years, I have learned how valuable it is to build a strong fire of inner presence. In my relationships and professional life as a massage therapist, acupuncturist and now coach, I noticed I would often be tired after communicating or working with a client. What I discovered was that my attention was often more on the person I was with than on my inner experience. It was like I would leave myself to connect or support another person. This was a huge Ah –Ha moment for me when I began to practice staying in myself with my attention while connecting with who I was engaging with. This shift was amazingly energizing for me and I felt more sensitive and available than ever before! For me this simple practice increased my intuition, availability and clarity. Since I discovered this in my own self, I have taught it to many of my clients, whom I noticed would also put more attention outside of themselves while in relationship.

Being at home in your body and cultivating your inner awareness is a radical step in activating to your full potential. The more home you are in your body and experience, the safer and happier you will feel when you are with other people.

What stops most people from staying present is a resistance to feeling painful emotions. The remedy is to always do your best to welcome and allow your feelings. Staying present with our feelings is no small task, especially if we were taught or trained not to feel.

This can be particularly true for men because the beliefs that are instilled culturally are very tenacious. Of course women have also been conditioned to believe that some emotions are OK to feel and others are not. Either way, we want to get to a place where we value all of our feelings and allow the space to experience them. This is not to say that we want to wallow in our feelings or go into a pit of heaviness and despair. If we are genuinely willing to feel and stay present with what is happening in our bodies, blocked energy will release and you will eventually feel lighter and more relaxed.

It is not important or necessary to know why we are feeling a certain way. Often our perception of where our feelings are coming from is not accurate. **In fact, many of the feelings and reactions that we may be feeling have**

roots in an earlier experience that is being triggered by the current situation.

Please reread the above line! What is essential is to validate, allow and express our emotions and to support others in doing the same. Expressing emotions is not about blaming, either. Directing anger or blame at others is not constructive or helpful.

The ability to effectively express and validate tender, loving emotions is how we maintain close personal relationships. In this case, "effective" means sharing intimate feelings with someone in an appropriate relationship, in a manner that's nourishing and constructive, and being able to respond affirmatively when the other person does the same.

Take the time to practice giving yourself and your close ones more space to feel. It is helpful to encourage others to pause and feel, instead of talking over the feelings that are moving through them. Very often I see my clients override their feelings with the story of why or what is happening. To encourage someone to simply feel and allow the emotions to express is the most helpful thing that you can offer to yourself or another.

Keys to Emotional Intelligence

Every Event is Neutral

Every event is neutral; this is your natural state. If you feel triggered, it is most often an issue from the past that needs to be addressed, felt, and acknowledged. This is part of an old wound that is crying out for you to love, accept, and let it go.

When Your Buttons Are Pushed

If you are feeling triggered emotionally by something or someone, you are likely to feel upset, angry, hurt, withdrawn, or depressed. This is your first clue to pause and pay attention to what is happening within you. This is the perfect opportunity to process and clear an old emotion/feeling that was never resolved inside of you.

Remember, any time you are *strongly* emotionally triggered by something, the reaction has roots in your past. It is rarely from the present situation. If you did not have a wound there, or feel an emotional charge there, you would not feel that much pain or anger. Think about when you feel angry. Where do you hold that energy in the body? You cannot change how you feel; how you feel is how you feel. This needs to be honored and acknowledged to allow it to be fully resolved.

> "*Appreciate your triggers. Appreciate what and whom triggers you. To highlight our pathways to greater wholeness, is a great gift.*"
> - Meredith Murphy

How to Accept Responsibility For Your Emotions

First, realize that you have the choice and ability to respond. Secondly, stop blaming, projecting, and judging others. Resist pointing the finger at them, saying they are doing this to you. Blaming others keeps you in the victim role. When each person accepts responsibility for his/her own feelings, you will share all of yourself from a non-judgmental, empowered space. Can you imagine what would happen on earth if everyone took responsibility for their attitude and how they feel? One of the most empowering things you can do is accept responsibility for how you react. Stop the cycle.

My intention here is to offer you this simple yet very effective empowerment tool that you can use on a daily basis. You can clear and transform issues very fast if you are willing to be conscious and feel your emotions (energy) fully, accept responsibility for your own feelings, and stop reacting to what triggers you, and projecting it out on to someone or something else. This is one of the most empowering things you can do for yourself. Choose to use your emotions as a tool to clear and liberate yourself into wholeness.

Notice Your Coping Mechanisms

You need to know how you cope and how you express your energy. Do you deny or suppress your emotions (saying you're fine, but feel like exploding)? Do you choose to hold on to a negative feeling and not express it? Do you carry it around like dead weight (the world on your back)? Are you feeling really tired all the time? Do you dump on another or blame someone else for how you feel? Knowing the answer to these questions will give insight into any unconscious patterns of avoidance you may be doing.

When You Feel Emotional What Do You Do?

What is your coping strategy? Do you go shopping, eat or overeat, drink or use drugs, clean the house, or be really busy to avoid looking at what you are feeling? Do you go to the gym and exercise like crazy, or go back to work so you don't have to think (feel) about what's up for you. What do you do to avoid yourself?

How to Process your Emotional Energy?

You have to be willing to go in and feel the pain. Feeling it is healing it. Is it going to be uncomfortable? Yes, it is. You have to be willing to feel the discomfort and the pain. When you do, the energy/emotion gets expressed and it naturally moves through you and creates space for new things to come into your life. If you are willing to take ownership of what you are feeling, you will experience a growing sense of power and clarity. Your life will expand from being a victim to a powerful co-creator.

Heart Based Communication

The number one complaint in most relationships is "I don't feel heard or understood." Successful relationships are made or broken by the ways in which you do and don't communicate with others. No matter your current level of skill, you can become even more effective in the ways you engage through your presence, listening and accountability to your word.

It is essential to develop the art and skills of masterful communication to help all your interactions become opportunities for mutual understanding, connection and intimacy. Most people have not been taught about healthy communication, nor has it been modeled for us, so there are not many reference points to depend upon.

For me this has been a consistent journey of seeing the ways that I would hold back my communication and feelings for fear of having them be made wrong or not accepted. When I was young, I was told that I was too sensitive and when I was upset, my mother would sometimes get uncomfortable and my father would get angry and intolerant. So I learned that it was not safe for me to express all of my feelings and I would control my expressions. Learning how to communicate authentically for me was a practice in cultivating trust in myself and seeing that what happened with my parents was not necessarily going to happen with my partner. Take a look back at your family environment, were all of your feelings and expressions welcomed? Or did you learn to hold back certain feelings that you may still be doing now?

Our words are only part of what we communicate. We send and receive energy from our hearts and minds all the time. We are all more sensitive than we realize. Every thought or feeling emits a frequency outward from our being. This is why we often know what our partner is thinking or feeling without them saying anything.

Our ability to sense this energetic information gets stronger when we are in a close relationship and when we put our attention on it. This is one of the many reasons why authenticity is essential for a healthy relationship. We have all experienced how confusing it can be when we receive mixed messages. Your partner is saying one thing and thinking or feeling something else that you can sense or perceive. We cannot truly lie in a relationship. The truth is always out, just not always spoken!

Heart based communication is a way of listening with your whole being and not just your mind. The mind/ego likes to take fixed positions of understanding for safety and security. However, safety and security are like a desert with no water when we are closed to intimacy and connection. Deep down, even when someone is frustrated and pushing away, there is a desire for love and acceptance. The origins of pushing away are usually from a hurt or wounded place that is attempting to protect and prevent a painful experience from repeating. When you understand this and penetrate through any defenses with loving acceptance, situations that were once conflicting can easily be transforming and healing.

In our Western culture, we are conditioned to communicate in ways that create a certain social etiquette or comfort. If you have ever been around native cultures, you will notice that they speak fewer words and allow more space for silence. They listen more than they speak, hearing the sounds of the environment, and are more highly tuned in to the subtle sounds and vibrations that are all around them. In contrast, we live in a fast paced and busy world that is centered around thought and doing. Our wider senses of awareness are underdeveloped, while assessing and thinking is overused.

A relationship can be a delightful place to slow down our minds and allow for a more rich and fulfilling experience of connection. With practice we can get more comfortable being close and intimate with fewer words and more connection. By slowing down and expanding our awareness, we can allow the communication of our hearts and energies to fill up the space between us. At first, this can be very challenging and unfamiliar and may bring up feelings of discomfort to the surface. This is a good thing. Many people have been conditioned to suppress feelings and avoid discomfort, which consumes energy and creates a subtle agitation that will not go away until the dam is removed and the feelings are freed to flow. If you allow space for this with breath and attention, you will find that your mind will slow down and you will become more sensitive and awake to all of the subtle energies that are present.

To cultivate more awareness and a calmer mind, try this practice:

Begin with focusing on and feeling the sensations around your chest and heart. Bring the attention of your mind down to your heart and welcome the sensations and experience of this area to light up. You can concentrate on breathing in and out of the heart to help calm your mind and bring more awareness here.

With your partner, you can sit across from one another or lie down heart to heart and focus on feeling each-others' hearts. This is a beautiful way of deepening your connection and turn on more loving feelings. It is also a powerful way to make amends and become close again after a challenging situation.

How to communicate clearly and resolve a disagreement

Conflict in a relationship is virtually inevitable. In itself, conflict is not always a problem; how it's handled, however, can bring people together or tear them apart. Poor communication skills, along with disagreements and misunderstandings can be a source of frustration and distance, or they can be a springboard to a stronger relationship and happier future.

When we are tuned in to the energy behind the spoken words and we are listening with our entire body and not just the head, a whole new dimension of communication becomes available.

One of the biggest obstacles in our life is the notion that we "know". We think we know what another person is saying or what they mean without being fully present and listening with our entire being. While this part of our human nature helps us in relating to one another by giving meaning and value to words, it can also become a limitation. If we truly want to hear each other, we have to be present with each other, by listening with fresh curiosity and openness to what is being spoken beneath the words.

Here are some ways that you can create more fulfillment and harmony in all of your interactions:

Stay With What Is Happening Now

Sometimes it's tempting to bring up past conflicts when dealing with current ones. Unfortunately, this often clouds the issue and makes finding mutual understanding and a solution to the current issue less likely. Moreover, it can make the whole discussion more taxing and even confusing. Try not to bring up past hurts or other topics. Stay focused on the present and stay aware of your experience and feelings.

Listen Carefully

People often think they're listening, but are really thinking about what they're going to say next when the other person stops talking. Truly effective communication goes both ways. While it might be difficult, try really listening to what your partner is saying. Don't interrupt. Don't get defensive. Just listen and reflect back what he or she is saying so they know you are clear about what they have said. Then you will understand them better and they will be more avaiable to listen to you.

Try To See Their Point of View

In a conflict, most of us primarily want to feel heard and understood. We talk a lot about our point of view to get the other person to see things our way. Ironically, if we do this all the time, there's little focus on the other person's point of view, and nobody feels understood. Make it a priority to really see the other side, and then you can better explain yours. (If you don't "get it", ask more questions until you do.) Don't jump to conclusions or assume that you "get it" until you really do. Others will be more likely to be willing to listen if they feel heard. This practice of listening and being heard is powerfully effective when it goes both ways.

Respond to Criticism With Empathy

When someone comes at you with criticism, it's easy to feel that they are wrong, and to get defensive as a result. While criticism is hard to hear, and often exaggerated or colored by the other person's emotions, it's important to listen for the other person's pain and respond with empathy for their feelings. Also, look for what's true in what they are saying; there may be valuable information for you to learn from their point of view.

Own What's Yours

Realize that personal responsibility is a strength. Effective communication involves admitting when you're wrong. If you both share some responsibility in a conflict (which is usually the case), look for and admit to what's yours. It diffuses the situation, sets a good example, and shows maturity. It also often inspires the other person to respond in kind, leading you both closer to mutual understanding and a solution.

Use I Statements

Rather than saying things like, "You really messed up here," begin statements with "I", and make them about yourself and your feelings, for example, "I feel frustrated when this happens." It's less accusatory, sparks less defensiveness, and helps the other person understand your point of view rather than feeling that they're being attacked.

Look for A Win Win

Either through compromise, or a new solution that gives you both what you want most, this focus is much more effective than one person getting what he or she wants at the other's expense. Healthy communication involves finding a resolution that both sides can be happy with.

Take a Pause and Breathe

Sometimes too much emotion or reaction is triggered, tempers get heated, and it's just too difficult to continue a discussion without it becoming an argument or a fight. If you feel yourself or your partner starting to get too angry to be constructive, or showing some destructive communication patterns, it's okay to take a break from the discussion until you both cool off. Sometimes good communication means knowing when to take a pause and shift the dynamic.

Don't Give Up

While taking a break from the discussion is a good idea, always come back to it. If you both approach the situation with a constructive attitude, mutual respect, and a willingness to see the other's point of view or find a solution, you can make progress toward the goal of a resolution to the conflict.

Ask For Help If You Need It

If one or both of you has trouble staying respectful during conflict, or if you have tried resolving conflict with your partner on your own and the situation just doesn't seem to be improving, you can benefit from a few sessions with a relationship coach or therapist. Couples coaching or family therapy can provide help with persistent issues and teach skills to avoid future conflict. If your partner does not want to go, you will benefit from going alone.

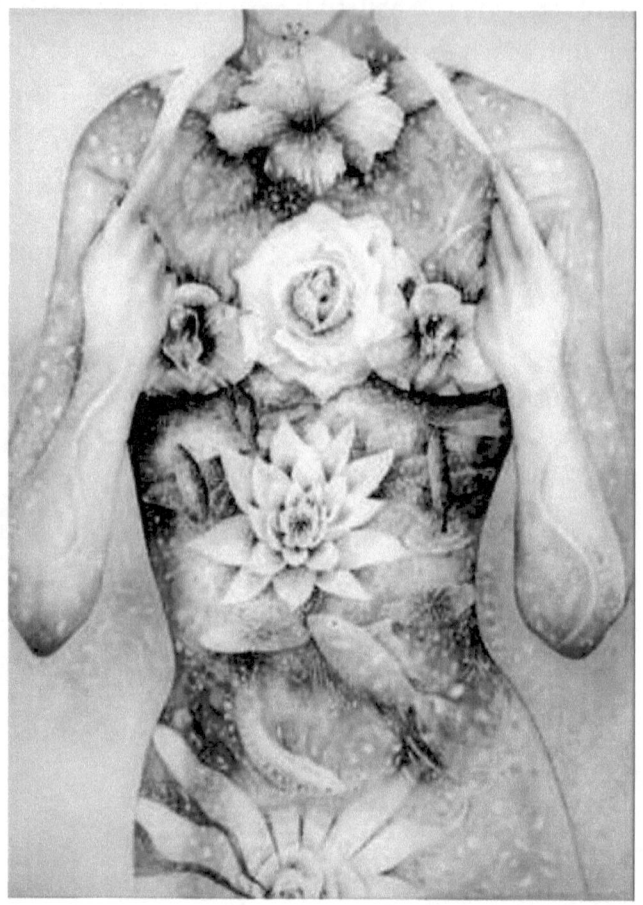

Radical Responsibility

You have far more power than you may realize to create the relationship you want. Taking responsibility for your own experience is sexy and enlivening. Who really is in charge of your state of contentment and happiness anyway? You get to choose to be the person you want to be and how you want to live. When you are consciously choosing what you want in relationship and aligning with it, you are the artist of your destiny. Radical responsibility is the fuel that can transform your life and the world around you.

Do you tend to want your partner to act differently or to change? This is a common mistake, and it pulls the plug on love. Your loved ones never signed up for a partner-improvement program! There is a reason that you have attracted the specific person or situation into your life. The path to freedom, inner power and even joy is in the practice of **taking 100% responsibility** for your life and relationship.

Being responsible is about harnessing the power of your attention and intention and putting yourself in the driver's seat of your life as the creator of satisfaction in all your relationships. Being aware of your thoughts, reactions and emotions, whether you respond or react is a conscious choice. Responding is feeling and acknowledging what is happening within you. Reacting is putting the attention out and blaming another, pulling away or getting defensive.

Blaming your partner for what is happening is not taking responsibility for the role that you play in the relationship dynamic. It can be tempting to blame your partner for the issues in your relationship. It's often easier to see what he or she is doing that is a problem than to look at yourself and your contributions.

When you put your attention or blame on the "other" or the outside events you are choosing to take the victim role. When you are in the victim role you believe that life is happening to you rather than **for** you.

Choosing to see that situations are happening **for** you to evolve is a radical shift in perception that can heal and change your experience of life in many ways. To see that life is happening **for** you rather than **to** you opens a doorway to using every situation as an opportunity to learn and grow. There is always a window of opportunity in every experience, no matter how painful and dark it may be.

The opportunities and challenges of life will never go away. We will all face constant change and eventually death. The key is to be willing to view all situations as blessings and opportunities, rather than burdens. Any unloved parts in ourselves will continually magnetize events and people that will give us the opportunity to choose to heal and integrate them.

It is your responsibility to generate the love and beauty that fulfills your life. It is your responsibility to choose to use the situations in your life as opportunities to grow and evolve. The ball is in your court! Are you going to fully participate in playing the most fulfilling game in this life? Do it and experience the thrill and energy of full participation!

Taking Responsibility

Here are some simple and effective ways to shift from outdated and limiting patterns into an empowered place of radical responsibility:

Be Honest and Authentic In Your Communication

If you feel angry, then say it and allow it to be there. There is no sense in hiding what is happening.

Stop Making Excuses

In any situation, there are always some factors we can't control. It is easy to blame those factors, or people, and vocalize them as excuses. Any time you make an excuse, it's like saying "I am not responsible for this because..." and what you're really saying is "I am not responsible." Pay attention to how you think and talk. Do you find yourself making excuses? Excuses come in many shapes and sizes, but the most common is "I would/would've, but..."

Admit Your Mistakes

If you never fess up to something you did wrong, then how can you learn from it? One of the key parts of accepting responsibility is being able to say, "I really messed up here. I won't do it again." Then be willing to acknowledge how your choice or action has affected your partner.

Do Not Blame Other People For Your Problems

Another way to accept responsibility is to stop putting the blame on everyone around you. Sure, life isn't fair and, unfortunately, some people have it rougher than others. You can blame your parents for not loving you enough and leading you down a dark path to an extent, but you won't be able to change the course of your life until you own up to your actions and make the changes you want to see in your life.

Stop Complaining

Complaining is another way of blaming the world for your problems instead of taking initiative and knowing what you can change.

Get Out of the Victim Role

The world is not out to get you. Even if you have had a traumatic life, there is good to be discovered through the challenges of your experiences. Even the worst tragedies yield diamonds that are hidden in the rough.

Accept What You Cannot Control

Though it's important to accept responsibility for your actions, it's equally important to understand that there are some things in life that are simply out of your control. There are three main files in life. The first one is your file and what you have control of. The second is other people's files that you can affect, but ultimately, have limited control over. The third is God's files, which are well beyond your reach. It is easy to put attention on other people's files and

God's files, while not taking advantage of what you have influence over.

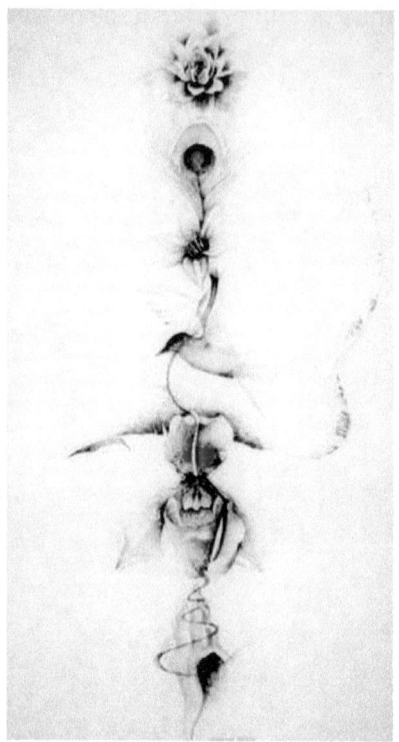

Self Mastery And Awareness

One of the greatest challenges in intimate relationships is the way in which your loved ones push your emotional buttons. Your partner says or does something you don't like, and you react emotionally, usually without even thinking. You may say or do things you regret later. This is called "triggering." When we are triggered, the first thing that most commonly happens is a tendency to be defensive. Defensiveness is the surest and most effective way to block love, intimacy and potential growth. On a biological level we activate the fight or flight survival response in the body.

Your emotional triggers are the clues that will help you to become more aware. Every emotional reaction has a feeling, thought or belief underneath it: self-doubt, anxiety, worry, fear, guilt, resentment, anger, shame, blame, depression, or loneliness. These arise from a "story" you tell yourself, and that you believe, whether consciously or unconsciously. Examples are: "I can't do this," "It's hopeless," or "I just don't think I am worthy." Most unconscious stories arise from some long ago childhood experience of trauma, abandonment, betrayal, or mistrust.

A contraction in your physical energy, a catch in your breath, a tightness in your chest, a sense of discontent, an anxious feeling in the pit of your stomach, these are giveaways, the tell-tale signs that you are caught up in **and** identifying with a thought or story. You can use these experiences to get curious within yourself to uncover what is really going on.

It only takes a moment to make a major shift from being stuck and defensive to being curious and willing. You make the choice to break the cycle by consciously breathing and feeling whatever is going on inside of you with loving acceptance and presence. In each moment that you choose to feel and be present with what you are noticing, you begin to metabolize and transform the blocks and unresolved wounds hidden deep inside. This is a powerful way that partners can support and love one other. To be present and loving with your partner through a wave of reaction or defensiveness, while encouraging one another to fully feel what is coming up in that moment is a powerful way to break old patterns and pain cycles. Sincere loving attention is one of the most powerful medicines in the world.

A Breathing Practice

Conscious breathing practices increase energy and support you to eliminate stress, anxiety and depression. By releasing suppressed emotions, awakening creative energies, and improving the immune system, deep controlled breathing will bring you into states of relaxation that encourage regeneration, healing and more pleasurable sexual experiences.

Various thoughts, feelings, sensations, and emotions will arise in the process of focused breathing. If you don't allow these things to distract you, if you don't make them important, if you don't react to them, and instead stay focused on relaxing and consciously breathing, you will observe that all those things naturally pass or fall away on their own.

The following breathing practice establishes a smooth continuous flow of energy and awareness in the body. This easy and natural breathing practice is also a gentle yet dynamic form of meditation.

In this simple breathing practice, the breaths are literally connected. That means there are no pauses or gaps between the inhalations and the exhalations. The in-breaths merge with the out-breaths, and the out-breaths merge with the in-breaths. Breathing is continuous; it turns like a wheel, smoothly, in an uninterrupted way.

Try it now:

Sit with your spine elongated, relax your body and give the flow of your breathing your undivided attention. Focus on the breath moving in and out gently, and keep it smoothly turning like a wheel. Connect your inhale to your exhale, and your exhale to your inhale, without any pauses or gaps between the breaths. No hesitating or holding the breath for a moment between the inhalation and the exhalation. And no waiting or resting between the exhale and the inhale.

The inhale is slightly active; the exhale is totally relaxed. Pull the breath in slowly and consciously; and let the exhale go quickly and completely. Ride the curve of the breath as it turns from inhale to exhale and from exhale to inhale.

Allow at least 10 minutes of this breathing pattern to flow before stopping. This will give the body and nervous system enough time to offload some tension and to rebalance your energy. You can do this practice anywhere and any time and it is best practiced sitting or lying down to allow for deeper relaxation.

You can also practice this with your partner before sharing intimacy to deepen your connection. Sit across from one another or lie down next to each other and allow the breathing to (take over) and expand your sensitivity. Or use it to release any blocks between you that are in the way of intimacy.

Everything Is Energy

Quantum physics tells us that nothing is actually solid.
Everything is energy. Everything is vibrating and
everything on earth is influenced by the movement of
energy. Plants grow better when exposed to certain musical
vibrations. Sound vibrations affect the form of molecules.
Words, thoughts and music affect the molecular structure
of water. The human body has a biofield of energy running
through and around it influencing and responding to our
mental and physical health.

We are energetic beings with true creative power and anything that clouds our knowing of this is an illusion and disempowering. Our nervous systems are amazingly sensitive and responsive to everything. Each thought we think sends out energetic information that attracts and affects that which shows up in our lives. We are continually interacting with the world through our unconscious or conscious thoughts and beliefs about reality. A lot of what we experience is unconsciously generating from the wounded and un-integrated parts of ourselves. Becoming more conscious through our attention and attitude is essential to attracting more of what we want and desire in our lives.

Most of what we are conscious of is only the tip of the iceberg; below the waterline of our awareness is a huge amount of information and experiences that are stored as energy in the subconscious. Knowing this is powerful! We have layers of impressions and experiences that have not been consciously integrated, ready to surface up to be transformed into usable energy. There is no need to understand why or what the unconscious stuff is about, you can simply think of it as raw energy that is ready to be transformed into usable fuel. This raw energy, in the subconscious, attracts situations and people that will help bring it to the light of conscious awareness. Any time that you welcome and allow for the full experience or emotion to be felt, you are allowing this raw energy to be refined and available for your life. It then turns into more passion, creativity and vitality that can be directed in any way you choose to.

Many advanced meditation practices have the intention to cultivate this ability to efficiently process this raw energy and utilize it for spiritual development and healing. In my Qi Gong training, I have practiced standing still in a meditative posture for an hour at a time. This was exceptionally challenging at first. My mind would go crazy and pain would show up in all sorts of places in the body. Sometimes I would feel nauseous or get headaches, feel angry and scared, it was very intense and difficult. Over time, standing and feeling energy flowing began to get easier. I did not understand what was happening until many years later, (Chinese teachers do not often say much about why or for what purpose you do the practices they teach).

What I came to understand is that this was a purification and strengthening process. I was surfacing all kinds of unprocessed energy that had been locked and held in my body and energy pathways. This was also waking up my ability to focus and harness my attention. It was training the mind to be still and present, (which most people know is not easy). Anytime we stop and really take time to be still and present with ourselves, we open up a pathway of awareness and experience that is highly beneficial. In my opinion, everyone can benefit from stillness practices that encourage developing sensitivity and awareness, while allowing all sensations or emotions to be felt and integrated.

In relationships, you synergize with the other person's energy, creating more energy than either partner can manifest on they're own. This is amazing; when you connect and resonate with another person it stimulates a soup of neurological impulses and biological activity that facilitate all sorts of responses in your body and emotional state. If you are sensitive to this, you can ride the waves of heightened awareness and pleasure as well as welcoming the unwanted feelings that may arise to be integrated. With practice the surge of emotions and energy being shared become a potent catalyst for sacred sexuality and profound intimacy.

Most people don't know how to stay present with the uncomfortable feelings that often arise or when things actually feel very good! People don't just have a threshold of tolerance for pain and discomfort, but we also have a threshold for how much pleasure they can feel. Everyone has a thermostat that regulates how much positive love and pleasure they can tolerate before hitting an unfamiliar or upper limit. This is one of the gifts of relationship; to consciously continue to raise the bar on how much positive experience we can sustain. Most relationships eventually get into a pattern of burning up the increased energy in power struggles and conflict, but with a few simple tools you can harness this energy and use it to generate more intimacy, creativity and pleasure.

You do this by using the moments that stimulate discomfort, fear or reaction as opportunities to take responsibility and to feel and heal the reactive parts with presence and love. Relationships tend to amplify both positive uplifting energy or the stuff that is in the way of it. The common tendency is to see the issues that surface up as problems needing to be fixed changed or altered. The cure for pain is in the pain ~ through your willingness not to fight what is emerging, but to create a space in the moment to allow it to surface, to be felt and transformed through acceptance and love, you become an Alchemist. The more skillful you get at this the smoother and quicker struggle and conflict dissolves. In this way, you free up more energy to intimately connect and expand your loving.

As energetic beings, we are very capable of transforming our experience with simple practices and exercises. Whether it is Yoga, Qi Gong, Breath-work or Meditation, these are all wonderful ways to enhance our life experience. The most important thing is realizing that it is relatively easy to enhance our experiences and to bring more light and positivity into our lives. The more skillful we are at influencing our energy in positive and uplifting ways, the better and more confident we feel. This is a big deal. When we feel energized, healthy and resilient, we are much better at being in a relationship. We can better handle the consistent stresses of children, work and family.

Taoist Yoga Practice

One of the most effective practices that I know of is consciously cultivating positive feeling states. It is also one of my favorite practices because it is such an easy, fun and very effective way to juice up your life experience. This practice helps develop healthy new neuro-networks that are generally under-developed in most people. These are essential to being able to function at a high level in the world. We only truly learn when we are relaxed and having a good time. When we put more attention on the positive, we break the spell that has us addicted to the familiar negative thinking patterns, which affect us in such profoundly limiting ways.

Try it:

Begin standing still, feeling your feet connected to the earth and the top of your head open to the sky. Next, begin Breathing into your belly and coming into a gentle rhythmic bouncing and shaking of your body from your feet up. Begin to think and intend each of these feeling states below. Use imagery and affirmations to activate a felt experience of each of these feelings. Take time for each one on the list below and go for at least 30 seconds to a minute.

The goal is to cultivate these feeling states in a way that you can physically feel. This will literally grow stronger neural connections that support positivity and empower your life. Do this practice daily and more than once a day if you can. This practice will promote the production of and flow of healthy responces in your body that are essential for a vibrant life. You can also do it sitting still and breathing. Most importantly, you want to feel the experience and notice the response in your body and energy levels. One of the best times to practice this is when you are stressed and wound up. Once you can shift your experience from stressful thoughts and emotions to a more open and pleasurable state, you will be well on your way to a more empowered and inspiring life experience. It is not intended to avoid feeling your feelings though. On the flip side, this is an effective way to saturate yourself with positive energy and feel good sensations that will balance out the tendency to get overwhelmed or overly stressed.

These are the five states to focus on and cultivate. Each one can elicit a significant experience. You can simply choose one of them, if you don not have a lot of time and it is best to fell all of them.

1. **Relaxation and calm** ~ feel your body relax and your mind slow down.

2. **Strength and an "I can do it attitude"** ~ visualize feeling confident.

3. **Joy** ~ feel happiness and gratitude throughout your whole body.

4. **Love** ~ think of who you love and how it feels in your body And feel love for yourself!

5. **Ecstatic Aliveness** ~ feel how alive all of your cells are, the pulsing of blood through your whole body and the miracle that is life!

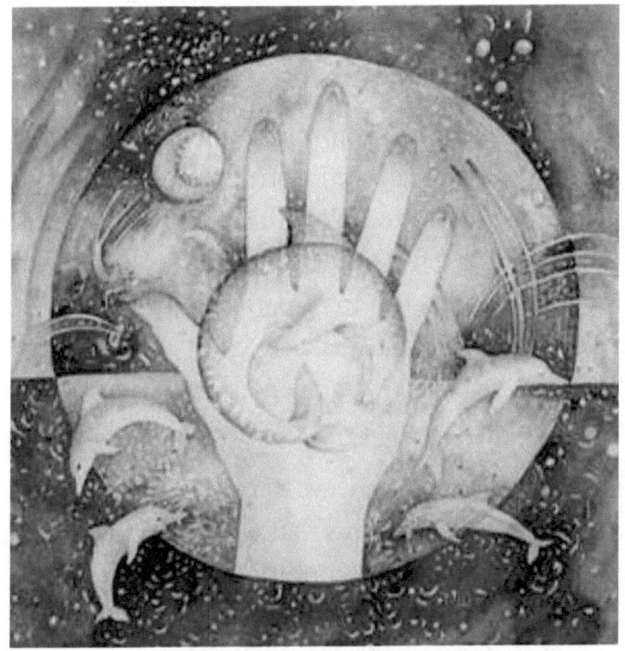

New Patterning

Have you heard it said that relationships are difficult and demanding? I think what is more accurate is that patterns of resistance and avoidance make everything in life difficult. It is a common story or belief that relationships involve hard work, compromise and settling for less than what you really want. This isn't necessarily true. We get to choose moment to moment how we perceive and react to what happens in our lives. The more we clear out the stories and reactions, the easier it gets to love and accept all the people in our lives. The bigger our story about struggle and difficulty, the more we will experience it. Ones attitude about life and relationships sets the stage for what will unfold.

Recycling relationship conflicts can be a form of addiction. If we grew up seeing struggle and fighting in our families then it is easy to follow that path, because it is what is most familiar. Even if we do not want to "be like our parents", it takes practice to re-pattern our unconscious behaviors. When you make a clear choice to end any form of addiction to struggle, you open up a new world of ease and harmony that you may not have imagined possible!

Each of us has certain ways of responding to new environments and situations that we established from our early childhood and social conditioning. We learned specific behaviors that helped us to feel safe with other people and challenging situations. For most of us, our responses and reactions from this patterning is unconscious and on a form of autopilot. For example: If my partner gets upset with me, I may get scared, withdraw my energy and pull away from her. I learned to do this when my mother was upset with me. The problem with this is that it is not what I want to do, but it is an unconscious response from past experiences.

Our actions will generally mirror what we observed from our early social imprinting with our families and social environments. When we choose to notice and pay attention to our responses and reactions we turn a light on in a dark room. With the light on we can see more clearly where we want to go with each step.

At first, it is easy to judge and try to push away the behaviors that we do not like or want. What is needed is to recognize and validate those behaviors and then to make a conscious choice to take a new step. In this way we will not build up a charge of avoidance or give power to what we resist. Forcing change does not bear long term fruit. It is through consistency and awareness that we consciously plant the seeds of what we most want. Loving awareness and compassion towards others and ourselves is the most effective way to support and encourage new behaviors. Anytime we make others or ourselves wrong for behaviors, shame creeps in and slows the process of learning and growing.

Shame has been used as a motivation in parenting, religion and education systems for a long time. Shame promotes feelings of not being good enough and does not foster healthy human development. Compassion is the antidote to shame. As it is with most poisons, the toxicity of shame needs to be neutralized by another substance. Compassion is the only thing that can neutralize shame.

Compassion is a powerful trigger for the release of oxytocin, the hormone that increases feelings of trust, calm, safety, generosity, and connectedness. Criticism, on the other hand, has a very different effect on our body. The amygdala, the oldest part of the brain, is designed to quickly detect threats in the environment. When we experience a threatening situation, the fight-or-flight response is triggered and the amygdala sends signals that increase blood pressure, adrenaline, and the hormone cortisol, mobilizing the strength and energy needed to confront or avoid the threat. Although this system was designed by evolution to deal with physical attacks, it is activated just as readily by emotional attacks—from others and ourselves. Over time increased cortisol levels lead to depression by depleting the various neurotransmitters involved in the ability to experience pleasure.

This is why it is so important to be gentle with others and ourselves when it comes to love and relationships. It is very difficult to learn when we experience criticism; it triggers shame and old patterns that sabotage self-love and acceptance.

For many people, it has become normal to be in a state of sympathetic response in the nervous system, which is commonly called fight or flight, and this supports reaction and defensiveness. Taking a moment to pause and relax your breathing during challenging times supports you to re-pattern the automatic response of fight or flight. An important practice in relationship is to learn how to sustain an open space of curiosity and wonder, activating the parasympathetic response, where we can digest and metabolize our experiences. In this way we create a safe container for intimacy and love to flourish like healthy plants in the sunlight.

Choose to use any moments of discomfort and reaction as doorways to greater discoveries and deeper intimacy. Not only with your partner, but especially with yourself. Each time you shift an old pattern you break a cycle that opens you up to greater possibilities.

Become Aware of Distractions

Everyone has his or her own way of handling stress, fear, sorrow and anger. We come to rely on various distractions to always be there for us when we need them. It is easy to get defensive and angry when these vices are threatened, not realizing the temporary comfort we seek in food, drugs, alcohol, shopping, the Internet, sex, or video games has actually been keeping us from our true happiness.

Only when we are able to bring loving awareness to our distractions, can we begin to break free of the self-destructive cycle. Nearly all of us have an experience or emotion that we have been avoiding in life. Fear, confrontation, shame, anger, and sadness are just a few examples. Nearly everyone has a raw nerve or uncomfortable situation we feel the need to dance around, an unconscious response that makes us flee to our comforting distractions. And it is these distractions or behaviors that keep us from feeling or thinking about what scares, torments, or annoys us.

Distractions are unconscious repetitive cycles of behavior that are often self-destructive and rob us of our life force.

Drinking, eating, shopping, gambling, working, the internet and social networking are all examples of potential distractions. We often hide in the darkness of our distractions and ignore the emotions surrounding our reality.

The bright side is that we can break the cycle and step into our brilliance if we choose to become aware of what it is we're running from and what we're running to. The key is awareness and acceptance. This is how we learn to create new patterns of behavior that nourish and enrich our relationships and personal power.

- What experience or feeling might you be avoiding?

- How do you deal with this energy when you have no choice but to face it?

- Take a breath and identify it honestly because when you come into an awareness of what it is, you can begin to dismantle the pattern of behavior.

- Be willing to Disrupt familiar patterns and reactions.

Awareness of the distraction allows you to be available for what's really transpiring inside of you. Connect with the feeling. Stop, breathe, and get present to what you're truly feeling. This is the conscious disruptor, the moment of truth that awakens you from any unconscious state of avoidance.

The conscious disrupter adds awareness to the unconscious cycle. Whenever you add awareness to a pattern that's unconscious, you're disrupting it --- stopping it in its tracks with mindfulness. You want to either disrupt it when you're in the behavior or preferably before the behavior happens. Recognize or embrace where you go, or what you go to when things get tough. Awareness is the key to disrupting your distractions and resourcing your peace.

A Way To Deeper Love

Love is the state of unconditional inclusion. Being a kindred spirit means using your relationship as an opportunity to awaken from the constraints and limitations of the ego. There are healthy aspects to our ego identity and limiting ones. The limiting aspects of our ego show up in the ways that we use differences and distinction to divide and separate us from our authentic expression of love. The healthy aspects of the ego give us free choice, individual expression and personal experiences. We are individuals in separate bodies and we are also fundamentally connected and far from separate.

To open to deeper love, we must peel away the thoughts and beliefs that are simply not true. The focus here is on emptying you out, so that you can make room for being occupied by the consciousness of unconditional love.

Relationship is a healing path, a sanctuary to recover from the illusion of separation. Using relationship as a mirror is a challenging practice, but one that can lead you into greater awakening. You'll find your ego's trickery exposed, which will allow you to awaken to the impact of your separation wounds and to take full responsibility in your relationships. There is no hiding in relationship; everything will eventually be exposed to our beloved. Many spiritual teachers will agree that relationship is a path that teaches us how to love and grow in the most profound ways.

Regardless of what your spiritual beliefs may be, this life is a sacred journey. All apparent obstacles and challenges are truly opportunities. Our willingness to grow through our resistances is the gateway to deeper love. When we are defensive and reactive, we are guarding and avoiding, which leads to disconnection and suffering. When we are heart-centered and available to give and receive love, we are having a profound impact on everyone and everything around us.

The universe reflects our inner state of thought and feelings back to us through the people and situations in our lives. If you focus your attention on the beauty and blessings in your life, you will experience a magnification of these.

Deeper Love Begins Within

Take moments to stop and be still. Empty yourself of the busy day-to-day life issues. Allow your busy self to unwind and expand into greater awareness and sensitivity. Choose to fill with joy, love and appreciation for no reason other than the fact that you can!

Life can sometimes feel like a train of busyness that you cannot get off. My remedy for this is to consistently take pauses. Every time that you bring your attention back to a wider awareness of your experience, you connect to a deeper place in yourself. That place is an experience of stillness and presence that is full of awareness. It is not your thoughts; it is an experience beyond thinking and doing. Not one that is easy to describe, but one that is fundamentally natural and beautiful.

Love is an experience, not a thought about experience. When you expand your awareness beyond thinking to encompass your whole being, you open up more dimensions of your reality. There is far more available for you to experience than you can conceive of. Use your breathing as a guide to sensing and feeling your body sensations, heart beating and the peace that is beneath everything. You can call this meditation or you can explore what it is and means to you beyond definition.

Any time that you enter into a deeper state of presence and awareness, you are expanding your capacity to feel Love. Trust me, if you practice this often your life will become more abundant and beautiful.

Bring this energy to your relationships and work place and see what happens.

Harness The Challenges

We are here to grow and evolve. Without pressure, diamonds do not form. The most rewarding experiences in life come from overcoming obstacles. Life's challenges carry hidden blessings within them. When I look back on my life, the rough patches are the times that have most influenced how I live my life now.

Some stress is good for us. The most influential artists and musicians will say that their masterpieces have come out of the depths of their hurt and longing. I believe that the treasures of life are buried in the burdens we carry. Our task is to make the most of what we have been given. To truly thrive we must turn our demons into art, shadows

into friends, fear into fuel and failures into teachers.
Harnessing the challenges in your life is a process of
alchemy and your attitude is the most important
ingredient.

Upsets

Mastery in relationships requires an understanding of
upsets. Freedom is always there within you as you realize
upsets aren't personal. Holding space for another's upsets is
terrific training in being present. It's the best remedy for
you, and the most loving act in any relationship.

Upsets are often about something other than what they
seem or something triggered from the past. If used
consciously as a tool for awakening, you can celebrate these
emotional experiences as opportunities for deeper
awareness and understanding with your partner.

Sometimes we do something or act in a way that hurts
or triggers another. When you apologize to your partner,
it's a powerful act of taking responsibility, which then
restores your own power. In every situation, taking 100%
responsibility is a potent place to stand. It offers you the
opportunity to be fully present in the moment with your
partner and frees you from the guilt or shame that can
linger in your psyche.

Expectations

It is a continual practice to let go of any expectations. Expectations can suck the joy out of your relationships and set you and your partner up for big disappointments. But when you can turn expectations into requests for what you want or what works for you, you'll find that your connection can be powerfully transformed, restoring love and intimacy. Our partners rarely know what we are thinking or what we most want. If you are not getting what you want, then choose to clearly ask for what you want and create the time to receive it. Often, people have inner blocks to receiving what they want. You may think that you desperately want something and then, when it shows up there is a fear or hesitation that can prevent it from happening. It comes back to each person's own awareness and responsibility to create what each most wants in relationship and life.

Cultivate Trust

Trust is so often overlooked in our efforts to find true partners and create intimate relationships that can truly last. It takes time to build trust – and actually requires the inevitable challenges and crises that come up in authentic relating. This is especially true if you are choosing to create an "empowered relationship" rather than a conventional model of relationship that often suppresses or deadens growth and change in each partner.

The most important trust to cultivate requires a strong belief in yourself and your capacity to learn and grow from all the challenges in your life. Every step we take toward shifting our attention from worry, fear and reaction toward letting go, intending and opening, strengthens and empowers our lives and relationships.

There is history of deep wounding in each of our family lineages. What humanity has created in the past is still echoing in all of us. Women have not been honored and respected in many cultures and there is good reason for men not to be trusted. Even now, there is massive violence and abuse towards women, animals and nature that shows the low level of consciousness and responsibility of humanity. It is our responsibility to transform these patterns from the inside out. In our personal lives and relationships, we can make peace that will have a positive influence on the rest of the world.

Building a Bridge of Trust

Many people carry residue from past hurts and losses that can get in the way of opening to deeper intimacy. If you have lost trust in your partner, then it is time to rebuild that trust.

The first step is to become fully aware of the nature and extent of the hurt you feel. If your hurt is dismissed, minimized, or denied, by yourself or others, then the wound is likely to fester and it is unlikely trust will be repaired. To ensure this does not happen, ask yourself the following questions: How deep is the hurt/pain you suffer? Does the betrayal trigger earlier hurts exacerbating the pain and suffering? Has the hurt lingered for days, months, or even years?

Second, the person that betrayed you must really see and acknowledge the hurt. Apologies like, "I'm sorry you feel that way," or "I didn't mean or intend to hurt you," are rarely sufficient and often stop the healing process before the hurt is really looked at and properly acknowledged. To ensure this happens, the one who betrayed you must not only take some responsibility for the hurt but also acknowledge the injury and show a feeling reaction commensurate with the hurt (remorse, compassion, upset, etc.). When there is no real acknowledgment and feeling response, you may rightly feel that the person "doesn't get it," and the trust will not be repaired.

Finally, learn, over time, that you can respond and take another step in relationship even after hurts and betrayals have occurred. This takes a new kind of trust—the trust in ourselves to be aware of our hurts, express our hurts, and address the injury and breach with our partner. Essentially, you are saying, "I trust that there are times you will hurt me and I will hurt you. I even trust that sometimes this hurt will be a breach of an agreement we have. However, I also trust that we can take steps to address these hurts and breaches and even turn the process, over time, into a strengthening of our relationship."

There are clearly some breaches that cannot be fully repaired.

I am not suggesting, for instance, that a person who is physically violated should "work it out." You alone will know if the bridge of relationship is irreparably broken. You must trust yourself to know this and act accordingly.

Forgiveness

We have all been hurt or have hurt another. How we choose to deal with our hurt has a radical impact on our entire lives. Forgiveness is one of the most powerful ways we can help to heal our relationships, communities and ourselves. Forgiveness does not make what has happened right, but it allows us to release and liberate the energy that has not been processed in our beings.

Another way to understand forgiveness is to visualize that you have a connection with another who you have not forgiven that is incomplete. If you are holding onto resentment, anger or hatred, you are literally exchanging energy with this person and losing some of your vitality. An

69

incomplete with another person is like a hole in a bucket that is losing precious water all the time.

After the wildfire burned our home and land, I invited a long time friend to come down from northern California to lead the rebuilding of our new home. Well, things did not go so well. The cost of building the home began to skyrocket and we learned many hard lessons. I had high hopes of building a low impact, sustainable home with Green everything and was creating a monster of a mess. Good intentions are not always enough. I learned that I cannot cross an ocean on a positive attitude and good intentions alone; I need to be a competent sailor and ocean enthusiast to navigate the stormy of the wild ocean. So I got a PhD in house building through experience. My friend led the journey as best he could and contributed to some major issues and problems that escalated until we hit an impasse. I was very angry and hurt during the process. I felt rage, guilt, shame and disappointment. My wife and I did our best to take responsibility and learn from the major challenges and financial stress while we stumbled up the climb.

I had made a poor decision to not hire a more experienced contractor who lived in the same town. I felt that I had lead our ship into rough waters and it really cooked me inside. What really ate at me most was that I could not forgive my friend for how things went down, while the house problems continued to pop up like wild flowers in the spring. I began to feel how this anger was burning me inside and preventing me from being close and loving with my wife or myself.

Finally, I reached out and got support from a therapist and did the necessary processing of my anger and forgiveness to move on. Through the process, I got to see that my reactions and feelings toward my friend had deeper roots with my father. I had a lot of anger that I had not confronted with my father and forgiveness to do with him as well. A lot of healing happened from that experience and I feel stronger and clearer because of it. One of the significant shifts that happened for me was that I no longer desired to tell the story of what happened and I was more interested in what was here and now happening in the moment. The story lost its grip on my psyche and I was freer to be happy in the moment.

When we forgive we help to release and prevent experiences from recycling. We also call our precious energy home to the present time and place that we are in now. Now is where life is truly lived. If we do not release and accept the past, then we are not able to fully move forward into the future.

Have you ever noticed that you become like your parents in many ways, even if you consciously resist and intend to behave differently? This is due to the energetic patterns of traumas and unfelt feelings that have not been consciously released. We literally absorb the vibration and experience of our parents. As children, we are like sponges that soak up the environments we are in and this often includes the unprocessed feelings and pain of our parents. A lot of what we feel and react to is not even ours. As you become more aware and skillful at allowing your experiences to flow through you without adding judgment or resistance, you will integrate and release the old energies from your being.

Forgiveness Practice

Here are eight steps to help you to forgive and make peace with what has happened in your life. The practice of forgiveness has been shown to reduce anger, hurt, depression and stress and leads to feelings of hope, peace, compassion and self-confidence. Practicing forgiveness is necessary for healthy relationships as well as physical health. It also influences our attitude, which opens the heart to kindness, beauty, and love.

1. Try to understand exactly how you feel about what happened and be able to articulate what about the situation is not OK. Then, tell a trusted couple of people about your experience.

2. Make a commitment to yourself to feel the feelings fully and give yourself the loving attention that will help you feel better. Forgiveness is for you and not for anyone else.

3. Forgiveness does not necessarily mean reconciliation with the person who hurt you, or condoning their actions. What you are after is to find peace. Forgiveness is a doorway to greater peace and understanding within yourself.

4.   Use the Hawaiian Hooponopono practice. It means to make right and is an ancient practice of healing and forgiveness. It is in essence a cleaning or washing practice. We repeat these four phrases below with the intention of taking 100% responsibility for our actions, for the actions of others towards us and for everyone else as well. It is simple and very powerful when done with a sincere heart toward anyone and especially our own self.

I love you
I am sorry
Please forgive me
Thank you

5.   In moments when you feel upset, consciously breathe and be aware of your body and its sensations. Try to relax and shift out of your body's flight or fight response. This will help you to integrate and heal the pain.

6.   Give up expecting things from other people, or your life, that they do not choose to give you. Remind yourself that you can generate hope, love, peace and prosperity and focus on feeling positive energy within you.

7.   Put your energy into looking for nourishing ways to get your needs met through cultivating healthy relationships. Instead of mentally replaying any hurt stories, seek out new ways to create what you most want.

8.   Remember that a life well lived is your best revenge. Instead of focusing on your wounded feelings, and thereby giving the person who caused you pain power over you, learn to look for the love, beauty and kindness around you. Forgiveness is about reclaiming personal power.

Conscious Sexuality

Intimacy and sexuality are the glue of a healthy
relationship. Unfortunately, in much of the world, sexuality
has been put into the shadows and viewed as a hidden act
that is mostly about physical pleasure. Sexual intimacy is
sooo much more than simply physical pleasure and
procreation. Sharing our hearts, bodies, fluids and breath

can weave a sacred and profound connection that is both empowering and healing.

Sex is a common source of anxiety for many couples. Plagued by the world of "shoulds" that permeates our mindsets regarding love and relationships, most people carry a host of unrealistic expectations into their sex lives. When sex fails to live up to the impossible ideal, you may assume that there's something wrong with your relationship or that you're with the wrong partner. "Sex should be effortless," the media says. "You should have wild chemistry right from the start," Hollywood espouses. These are among the many myths that seep into our consciousness and can have a deleterious effect on our sex lives.

Many men are dependent on fantasy and visual stimulus for their sexual functioning and this is not healthy or normal. The tragedy for men is that porn images portray sexual ejaculation as the main outcome of sexual sharing and they often miss the deep pleasure of the slow building of powerful waves of pleasure with a beloved that does not even require ejaculation. Pornography, movies and television only show one branch of sexuality. There are many branches on the tree of intimacy and ways to deepen love and connection. The visual stimulus of objectification with women has lead to a lack of true and deep communion.

The truth is that sex is complicated. It touches on our most vulnerable places in every area of self: emotional, psychological, physical, and spiritual. Few people begin their relationships with a clean slate but arrive with negative experiences around sex, early trauma, and/or erroneous beliefs that color their sexuality. The bedroom is often the place where the past collides with the present, so it would make sense that it isn't always the smoothest ride. Getting comfortable with a sexual partner is an experience that builds over time. Even if your relationship began with powerful sexual fire and deep intimacy, you may reach times when the fire dwindles or life's stresses drain your passion. It is at these times when intimacy and connection can be the best medicine for our lives.

There is a pervasive confusion about sex and intimacy. We use the words interchangeably, but plain physical intimacy does not necessarily bring a meaningful experience or a sustainable connection. The more we focus on the physicality of sex—how we look, our performance and techniques—the further we get from true intimacy. When we cultivate a sense of appreciation with devotion and full attention to our partner, we enter into realms of deeper intimacy and bonding. With a strong connection of presence and intimacy we can travel into any aspect of sexuality and have it be deeply satisfying and meaningful. The moments that we are feeling deeply intimate lend themselves to experiences that generate long lasting waves of happiness and satisfaction.

Here are some suggestions and practices for cultivating deeper int_____ in your sex life. There is a focus here on _____ and presence with each other and less on ____te aspect of sexuality. Both are equally ____ be that your relationship needs more ____d powerful sexual experiences. If so, then use the foundation of the practices below to establish the intimacy that can support you in creating all that you desire in your sexual sharing.

Less Talking and More Experiencing

Often when we think of intimacy, we think about the sharing of our experience or secrets. There is something intimate about verbalizing our innermost thoughts and desires – especially when it comes to sex. However, as alluring as fantasy can be, by its very definition, it's a way of escaping reality. And we tend to hide behind our words, using conversation as a means of avoiding vulnerability. We tell people who we are instead of showing them.

True intimacy with a lover happens in the silent moments of presence and connectedness between words.

> **Practice #1:** Set a specific time to meet in the bedroom without speaking a single word. Spend an hour together, not talking, before any physical intimacy begins. Show up clean, physically and emotionally. This is an opportunity to let our stories fall away --- as individuals and as a couple --- making room for a deep, non-verbal, energetic connection.

Focus on the Subtle Pleasures and Let Go of Any Need to Orgasm

Pleasure is like an untapped resource that is begging to be explored. Orgasms are wonderful, but it's easy to overlook a whole frontier to explore that is filled with riches, when we wander through our loving instead of aiming to get somewhere. It is now widely understood that women can have over a dozen different kinds of orgasms.

From the time men are boys, they are fascinated with ejaculating, the experience is a built-in biological preoccupation. My experience has been that the more I open up to experiencing whole body sensations, the more pleasure I feel. Experiencing whole body pleasure and ecstasy is a real possibility for both men and women. We have misunderstood the destination of sex to be orgasm; and, by doing so, robbed ourselves of some potentially powerful opportunities for both pleasure and intimacy.

Practice #2: Agree upfront to forgo reaching orgasm. Take the possibility completely off the table, for both of you. By doing so, you provide space to be present and find appreciation of each moment for the pleasure and connection it brings, without distraction. Take turns bringing each other close and backing off. Notice the powerful bond created as you hold each other on the brink of ecstasy.

Go Slow, Breathe and Feel

We live in a fast-paced, over-stimulating, mentally active world. As a culture, we are usually focused on "doing" rather than "being." Because we juggle so many responsibilities, it is not always easy to shift gears and bring the engine to a purr. Choose to make your sexual intimacy your medicine.

> **Practice #3**: Create a bubble of time and space to climb into together. Do whatever it takes to enable getting lost in your own world together. Make a conscious decision not to rush. Let energy flow between you like a lava lamp. Moving verrry slowly, savor each moment of sensation and allow intimacy to rise like a building wave.

Breathe Together

One of the practices during sexuality is to turn the focus from thoughts to the breath. In Tantra, partners will "match breath" as a way of forming an energetic connection that is not based on the giving and receiving of physical pleasure.

> **Practice #4**: Begin in a simple embrace. Spend a few minutes slowing and synchronizing your breath. Silently negotiate a rhythm that is comfortable for both of you. Pause at the top of each inhale and at the bottom of each exhale, creating a moment of mutual stillness. Breathing together is facilitated by

cooperation and consideration for each other. Try to maintain this collaboration during your waves of pleasure and experience.

Take Moments to Look Deeply Into Each Others Eyes

Eye contact is a distinct point of connection. Yet, it is common to keep one's eyes closed during sex. Extended eye contact reveals vulnerability, and so it can be a powerful facilitator of intimacy.

> **Practice #5:** Sit on the floor facing each other and gaze into each other's eyes without looking away for 20 minutes. Shifting from eye to eye helps sustain the gaze. Maintain eye contact as much as possible as sex unfolds. Play with looking into each other's eyes all the way through orgasm. It is nearly impossible to climax with open eyes (like sneezing).

> Gazing into your lover's eyes at the moment of release just might be the very definition of intimacy.

Amplify your pleasure

All kinds of healthy chemicals are stimulated throughout our bodies when we feel good. The adrenal glands that produce the stress hormone cortisol actually respond to brain messages originating from the heart, which is well supplied with neurotransmitters. This is why positive emotions and the release of oxytocin are vitally important for reducing stress. When you love your partner and surrender into deep pleasure and orgasm, you are replenishing and nourishing yourself on a cellular level.

> **Practice #6:** Focus on what feels good and allow your attention to feed the experience. Welcome sound, moaning, breathing and groaning. Let yourself be a glutton for what feels good and a willing giver of pleasure to your beloved.

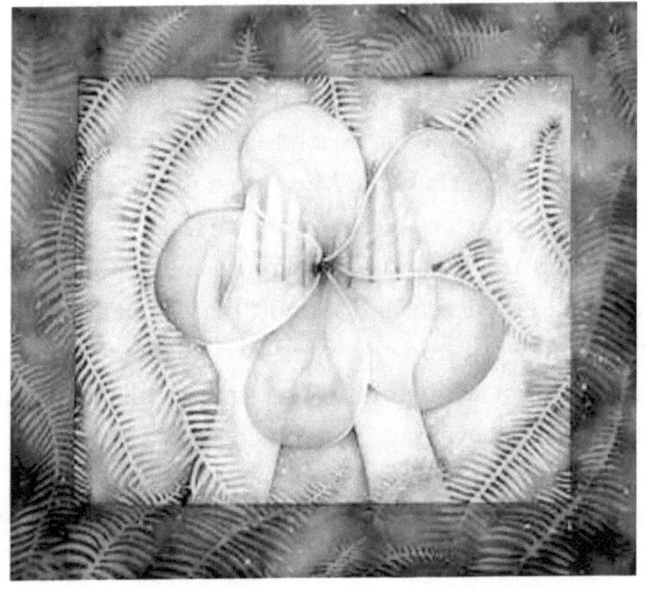

Get Support

I am sharing this work because I have received wonderful guidance and support in my relationships and along my journey. I would love to see every couple choose to explore body-centered forms of coaching or therapy to strengthen and deepen their relationships. We all need positive role modeling and encouragement to release unconscious patterns and create new ways of responding to the triggers and habitual tendencies that we learned from our families and society. In my opinion, the best way to discover our blind spot is to have a third party witness who can shine light on our shadows. In a safe environment, we have the ability to see things more clearly, with less reaction and more curiosity and this is the key to opening new doors of possibility.

My experience has seen that it is extremely helpful to have a skillful therapist or coach to help bring awareness to our unconscious behaviors. Most often we are not able to receive our partner's feedback until we learn to dismantle our defenses and expand our openness to learning. This usually takes modeling and support that happens in sessions and workshop environments. There are many great workshop facilitators and seminars available that are actually fun and exciting. You can check out what I offer or work with me privately by going to my website: shemsheartwell.com. I offer private retreats for individuals and couples who would like to experience rapid transformation and empowerment on the island of Maui. I also highly recommend the work of Gay and Katie Hendricks: hendricks.com.

In Conclusion

My hope is that the material in this book has been valuable to you in many ways. May your journey of loving be a rich and ever expanding tapestry of experiences. It is through consistency that we create new patterns and it can be difficult to stay on track sometimes. What I have found in my life is that I learn quickly and forget easily if I do not make something a priority. For me, understanding is only one part of learning. The most important aspect of knowing comes through regular experiences that activate the nervous system in a process of whole body learning.

When we engage our whole body in learning we grow rapidly. So please, as often as possible, slow down and expand your attention into your whole body and be aware of the signals that are always there to inform you. Your breathing, tensions or emotions are there to guide you. When you listen, you will hear and discover. Feeling is a form of healing that goes a long way in relationships. Every time we drop in to our body experience and out of the busy mind, we open up a vast potential for healing, growth and transformation.

I am a passionate learner and welcome your feedback. If you would like to share it, please send an email to shems@shemsheartwell.com

Aloha ~

Shems

Copyright 2015